Blessings Emma
Katie Reynolds Eph 3:20

Shannon Kincaid ♡

AT THE Water's EDGE

written by
KATIE W. REYNOLDS

illustrations by
SHANNON KINCAID

Copyright © 2012 Katie W. Reynolds

All rights reserved. No part of this book may be used or reproduced by any means, graphic, electronic, or mechanical, including photocopying, recording, taping or by any information storage retrieval system without the written permission of the publisher except in the case of brief quotations embodied in critical articles and reviews.

WestBow Press books may be ordered through booksellers or by contacting:

WestBow Press

A Division of Thomas Nelson
1663 Liberty Drive
Bloomington, IN 47403
www.westbowpress.com
1-(866) 928-1240

Because of the dynamic nature of the Internet, any web addresses or links contained in this book may have changed since publication and may no longer be valid. The views expressed in this work are solely those of the author and do not necessarily reflect the views of the publisher, and the publisher hereby disclaims any responsibility for them.

ISBN: 978-1-4497-5810-3 (hc)
Library of Congress Control Number: 2012912374

Printed in Canada by Friesens
Altona, Canada
October, 2012
79585

WestBow Press rev. date: 10/05/2012

For my precious children
George, Ben, Catherine, and Luc

It was midsummer and time once again for my mom, dad, two brothers, and little sister to pack our bags and head for our annual beach trip to Georgia. Dad and Mom figured out the details while we kids began chattering about all the fun things and adventures that lay ahead.

We thought about the jeep train ride to the end of the island, where Dad picked up a crab with his bare hands and we played in the tide pools.

We could almost smell the cinnamon butter on the rolls at our favorite restaurant and could hardly wait to order chocolate sundaes at the ice cream parlor.

We have been going to the same beach my whole life. Even my grandfather went there when he was a little boy. A long time ago He and my grandmother celebrated their honeymoon at this beach. As I dressed for the trip, I realized what a special place this was for my family and had been for many years.

This summer something incredible happened! In my big family of six, I was really wanting a one-on-one, warm, fuzzy moment with my mom. You know, the kind when you are the center of her world and nothing else matters. So as soon as we got there, I asked Mom to go for a beach walk—just the two of us. It happened, and hand in hand, we began a beach walk I'll never forget.

As we stepped onto the beach and squished the sand between our toes, big smiles filled both of our faces. I said, "Mom, I wonder if I could find a conch shell this year, a big one with no cracks that I could take home and keep." Mom replied, "Honey, why don't we ask God to give you a shell? Nothing is too small to ask Him. He can do more than we could ask or imagine." So Mom and I said a simple prayer and praised God for His creation.

As I looked down at the beach, I could see our trail of footprints in the sand and only small, broken pieces of shell scattered on the beach. The thought of a whole conch shell began to look a bit impossible. We wandered down to the water's edge and began to kick around in the surf, hoping to find something there, when along came a lady with pretty auburn hair and a sweet smile.

She was carrying a clear plastic cup, and right inside you could see them! She had found two large shells, one a scallop and the other a conch. Mom and I politely passed by her with growing hopes that God might really answer our prayer. Our eyes gazed downward again, searching in the ebb and flow of the ocean.

All of a sudden, we heard someone calling to us. It was the lady with the shells! She seemed excited to share with us some great news. She asked my mom if she could give me something and said God had a present for me. Mom grinned as the Lord began to unfold the answer to our prayer.

The lady knelt down and placed in my hand a large conch shell—the one she had been carrying in her cup. She said the Lord God wanted me to know He created the world and everything in it, and He had asked her to give the shell to me. She told me to never forget this and to keep the shell as a reminder of Him and His creation.

Mom and I marveled at our great and caring God. Then we told her about our prayer. I watched as she and my mom shared tears, not sad tears, but joyful ones. Thinking this was good-bye, we thanked our new friend and continued on our walk together—just Mom and me ... and God.

We began to thank Him by singing:

God is so good; God is so good;
God is so good; He's so good to me.
He answers prayers; He answers prayers;
He answers prayers; He's so good to me.

Moments later, we heard our new friend calling to us again. She was running back down the beach toward us. Her hair was flowing in the wind, her eyes were filled with excitement, and she was waving something huge in the air. It was another conch shell—the biggest one I had ever seen!

The Lord had given her a present too—a reward. You see, she had wanted to keep the shell for herself, but God wanted her to give it to me. He wanted to use her to answer my prayer. She put away her own desire to keep the shell and obeyed His leading to bless someone else. Because of her obedience, God brought blessings to us all!

At the water's edge, where we had just walked, the Lord had provided for her an even bigger conch shell than the one she had given to me! She leaned over and offered me the larger one. It was so heavy! I held on to it with both hands. It was smooth underneath and bumpy on top.

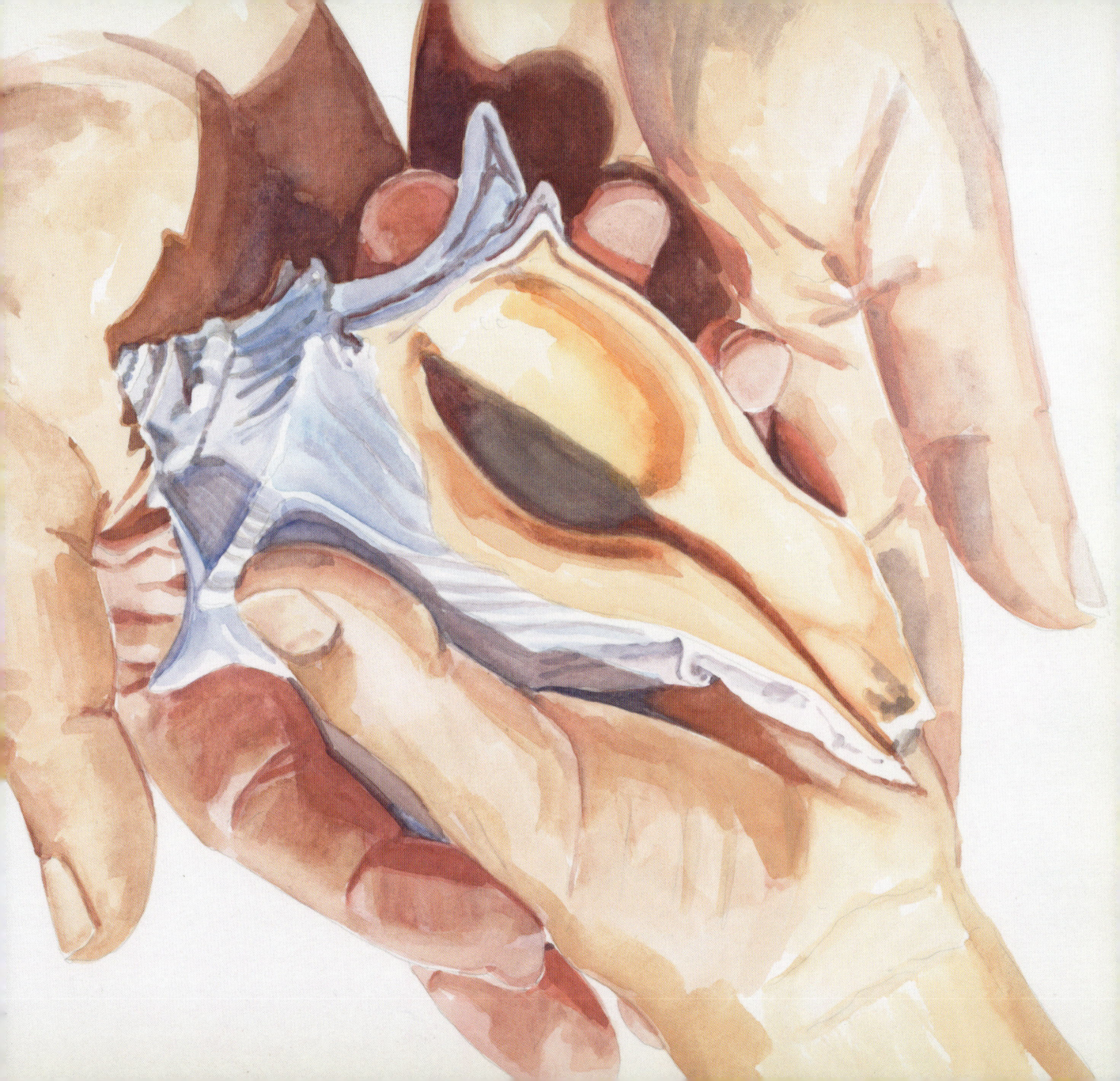

I held it up to my ear and heard the mighty rumble of the ocean. It made me think of God's power. I felt in my heart the love of my heavenly Father. He cares for me. He heard my prayer and answered me – in a way greater than I had ever imagined.

Intentional points from the story to *grow intimacy* and draw your family to the *heart of God.*

- Use your life experiences to strengthen your family's belief system that is built on biblically based convictions.

- Prioritize ways to make each member of your family feel valued.

- Respond to your child's needs for intimate quality time.

- Build faith by engaging your child to pursue his or her desires through prayer so he or she will see the kindness of God.

- Train your child to respond to the leading voice of God and prepare him or her to carry out His ways.

- Encourage your child to recognize that temporary treasures are best surrendered for eternal reward.

- Challenge your child to be a vessel for His glory by responding to the needs of others.

- Model and praise an obedient heart that brings about revelation and blessings.

- Lead your child through sacrificial giving, and open the door to receive God's blessing.